BENWELL 1o CHESTERS IN THE DAYS OF THE ROMANS

by
Frank Graham

Illustrated by
Ronald Embleton
(Vignettes by Gill Embleton)

I.S.B.N. 0 85983 147 7

1982

Published by
FRANK GRAHAM
6, Queens Terrace, Newcastle upon Tyne, NE2 2PL

Printed by Howe Brothers (Gateshead) Limited

BENWELL TO CHESTERS

Just over two miles west of Benwell fort the modern traveller gets his first glimpse of the Roman Wall in situ. Two stretches are visible on his left as he goes up Denton bank.

Where the wall crossed Denton Burn there could still be seen in Bruce's day a Roman culvert which he described and illustrated.

"The circular arch is the drain which was formed when the road was made. The Roman channel is beneath. It consists of two lines of massive stones laid parallel to each other, about two feet apart. The top was covered over by other large blocks, giving the conduit a height equivalent to its breadth. This seems to have been the usual way of allowing brooks to pass the Wall."

CENTURIAL STONES FROM THE VALLUM

West of Denton Burn in 1936 six centurial stones were discovered in the Vallum when a new road was being built. They were set in the mounds to the north and south and looked on to the berms. They were all alike, thin slabs about three inches thick on which the *centuria* had inscribed its official title. This was the first discovery to show that the Vallum as well as the Wall had centurial stones. From the discoveries near Denton Burn we now know that the Vallum was built in sections about 100 yards long, the work being done by centuries, from the auxiliaries as well as the legionaries. Each century was entirely responsible for its section and marked the completion of its task by two identical inscriptions on the north and south mounds. At Denton the work was done by centuries of the Second Legion and the First Cohort of Dacians. The most interesting stone is the one shown on our drawing. It reads:— COH.T DACOR(um) (centuria) AEL (i) DIDA (e) — *First Cohort of Dacians, century of Aelius Dida.*

The second element of the centurion's name DIDA is thought to be Dacian. The name Aelius is from the praenomen of the emperor Hadrian during whose reign Dida must have received his Roman citizenship.

The Works at Heddon-on-the-Wall

Between Denton and Heddon on the Wall little is to be seen today but at Heddon we encounter the Military Road, a work of immense importance to the Wall, since its construction led to the overthrow of a large section of the mural barrier.

The history of the Military Road is well known.

During the Jacobite revolt of 1745 the Pretender's forces advanced down the west coast. General Wade, stationed at Newcastle, was unable to advance on Carlisle because there was no good road along which he could transport his artillery, and the city was lost. To avoid a similar contingency in the future the "Military Road" was built and a large section of the Roman Wall was destroyed.

The Northumberland section was started in 1752 and completed five years later.

From Heddon the Military Road runs east in an almost straight line. The older road to Corbridge (A69) turns off to the south and follows a winding course. Travelling along the Military Road today one can see, for long stretches, the wall ditch to the north and the Vallum to the south. The road generally runs on the Wall foundations.

Milecastle 13 which is the nearest to Vindobala (Rudchester) is visible.

Towards the end of the occupation of the Wall one can imagine the troops at Vindobala were in a state of nervousness expecting an attack any day. At some point the fort commander must have decided to hide some of the cohort's money in case the fort was overrun. Beneath the floor of the nearest milecastle the money was hid temporarily (or so it was thought) almost fourteen hundred years later the hoard was uncovered.

In the castellum nearest to VINDOBALA, on the east, two poor labourers, in 1766, found a small urn full of gold and silver coins, 'almost a complete series of those of the higher empire: among them several others: most of them in fine preservation.' At first a quantity of them were dispersed about Newcastle; but Mr. Archdeacon, the proprietor of the estate and mesne lord of the manor 'claimed them as treasure trove, and recovered nearly five hundred silver and sixteen gold coins'; though he in turn, after proceedings at law, was compelled to deliver them up in the court of Ovingham to the Duke of Northumberland, the chief lord of the fee.

RUDCHESTER FORT (Vindobala)

Rudchester, the fourth fort from the eastern end of the Wall, lies 6¾ miles from Benwell. It was garrisoned in the fourth century by the First Cohort of Frisiavones the name of a tribe from what is now the Netherlands. In the *Notitia* it is called *Vindobala,* in the *Ravenna* List *Vindovala.* In the second century the garrison was probably cavalry, the fort having been built by Hadrian for a *cohors quingenaria equitata.* Towards the end of the second century it was burnt down but shortly afterwards rebuilt. A century later it was abandoned for reasons unknown, and about 370 A.D. it was re-occupied and restored and continued in occupation for a long time.

Opposite. General Wade's Army advancing along the old "Heeway" to Hexham in 1745.

4

Roman soldiers burying money

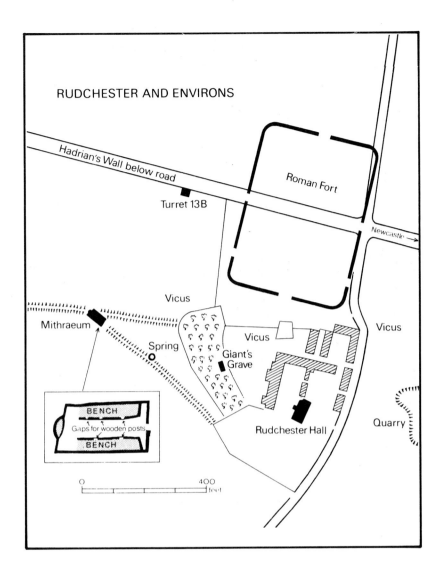

RUDCHESTER AND ENVIRONS

Hadrian's Wall below road

Turret 13B

Roman Fort

Newcastle →

Vicus

Mithraeum

Spring

Vicus

Giant's Grave

Vicus

BENCH

Gaps for wooden posts

BENCH

Rudchester Hall

Quarry

0   400
         feet

Apart from brief mention by Camden the first description of the fort is by Robert Smith (1708):

On the south side of the Wall, are visible ruins of a very large square Roman Castle, with foundations of several houses in the middle of the area: the square, as nigh as I can guess, may be about one hundred and fifty yards; and at the west part of the square are three or four plots of ground in the very Wall (which seems to have been five or six feet thick) for little Towers. This has also a Vallum round it, and joins close to the Wall.

The last account of Rudchester before the military road was built is from Horsley's *Britannia Romana* 1732.

"This fort has been very considerable, as the ruins of it at present are very remarkable. On the north side there have been six turrets, one at each corner, one on each side the gate, and one between each corner and those adjoining to the gate. On the east and west sides there is also a tower between the gate and the

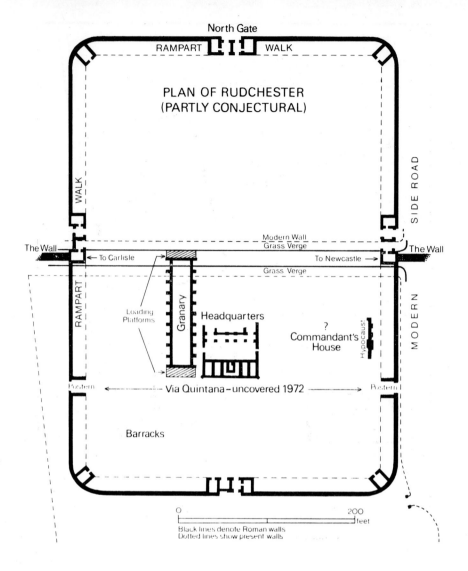

North Gate

RAMPART   WALK

PLAN OF RUDCHESTER
(PARTLY CONJECTURAL)

WALK

SIDE ROAD

Modern Wall
Grass Verge

The Wall   The Wall

← To Carlisle   To Newcastle →

Grass Verge

RAMPART

MODERN

Loading
Platforms

Granary

Headquarters

?
Commandant's
House

Hypocaust

Postern   Postern

←— Via Quintana – uncovered 1972 ——→

Barracks

0   200
feet

Black lines denote Roman walls
Dotted lines show present walls

angle, in that part of the fort that is on the north side of the wall; but 'tis doubtful whether there has been the same number of towers in that part that lies within the wall. At present however they are not so distinct.

The ramparts of this fort are still very visible, being in the second degree or more on everyside. The ditch is but feint, and scarce discernible on the east side, being levelled in the highway. On the other three sides it is visible. The ruins within the fort plainly appear, and the entries into it may be distinguished. If there has been a town without, which there can scarce by any doubt of; it has been as usual on the south, where the village of *Rutchester* now stands, and covers its ruins."

William Hutton (1801) describes how:

What remains is a close, joining the road, of five acres, now in grass, and eminently situated; carries the strong marks of former buildings, and still stronger of its ramparts. The platform of this grand Station is complete. I have all along inquired for turrets; but might as well have inquired among the stars. I was given to understand, that part of one was remaining here.

Fireplace at Rudchester Hall

The farmer was not helpful and made a jingle in his honour.
I saw old Sir at dinner sit,
Who ne'er said, "Stranger, take a bit,"
Yet might, although a Poet said it,
Have sav'd his beef, and rais'd his credit.

The fort measures 515 by 385 feet and covers 4½ acres. Little is to be seen apart from mounds to the south of the Military Road marking the west and south ramparts.

The building of the Military Road and the growth of agriculture in the eighteenth and nineteenth centuries led to systematic despoliation of the fort for its stone. The farm and house to the south and many field walls are built of Roman stones.

The first real exploration of the fort was carried out in 1924 and later in 1962. Two of the main gateways were excavated, a large granary and part of the principia were revealed, and a hypocaust belonging to the Commandant's house was discovered.

The Wall joined the fort at the main east and west gates leaving the gate passages to the north. The Wall Ditch existed before the fort was built. The west gateway which led on to the berm of the Wall was walled up but the date is uncertain. The thresholds show no sign of wear but since it was rarely used by wheeled traffic the closure might have been late in the Wall's history.

The south gate had an unusual arrangement. The west guard chamber was entered from the north and faced into the fort probably to control traffic going out. The other guard chamber had its door leading onto the gate passage as was normal. Early on the west portal was blocked and changed into a guard chamber.

9

At the same time the east portal was furnished with two inner gates.

When the Headquarter's building was excavated the wide middle chamber contained the usual strong room. Coloured plaster showed the room had once been decorated. The site marked hypocaust was probably the Commandant's house and bath-house. The wall shown has large buttresses.

The Vallum passes some 240 yards to the south of the fort while the vicus lay to the south and south-west. The "Giant's Grave" 95 yards south of the south-west angle of the fort is probably connected with a military bath-house not yet revealed.

Five altars (one of them uninscribed) were found to the west of the Giant's Grave. Four are here reproduced. They belonged to the Mithraeum which was

Size, 4 ft. 1 in. by 1 ft. 6 in.

DEO
L.[VCIVS] SENTIVS
CASTVS
LEG. VI. D[ECVRIO] ? P[OSVIT]²

To the god [Mithras]
Lucius Sentius
Castus
A decurion of the sixth legion erected
[this].

DEO INVICTO
MYTRAE P. AEL.[IVS]
FLAVINVS PRAE.
V. S. LL. M.

To the invincible god
Mithras Publius Ælius
Flavinus the præfect
most willingly
and fittingly
discharges his vow.

Size, 3 ft. 6 in. by 1 ft. 8 in.

Size, 3 ft. 4 in. by 1 ft. 7 in.

DEO SOLI INVIC[TO]
TIB. CL. DECIMVS
CORNEL[IA] ANTO-
NIVS PRAEF[ECTVS]
TEMPL[VM] RESTIT[VIT]

To the god the sun unconquerable
Tiberius Claudius Decimus
Antonius of the Cornelian tribe
the prefect
this temple restored.

SOLI
APOLLINI
. . . .

To the sun
Apollo

. . . .

Size, 3 ft. 7 in. by 1 ft. 5 in.

completely excavated in 1924. Two buildings were revealed both in the traditional style and shape. The date of the second building can probably be dated shortly after the destruction of Hadrian's Wall in 197 A.D.

The present Rudchester Hall is to outward appearance eighteenth century and the remains of the medieval tower can only be distinguished by the thickness of the walls. In the house is a remarkable fireplace here illustrated. The inner fireplace with stone lintel and carved jambs has at the bottom a Roman Cohort and Centurial Stone from the Roman Wall which recorded the work done by the Third Cohort of the Century of Pedovius.

Size, 1 ft. 6 in. by 7 in.

A centurial stone found at Rudchester. It reads (CO)H IIII   PEDI QVI – "the century of Pedius Quintus of the fourth cohort".

RUDCHESTER to HALTONCHESTERS

From Rudchester to Haltonchesters the Wall was practically destroyed by the builders of the Military Road. The Reverend William Stukeley in *Carausius* (1757-59) was incensed at the destruction wrought by "these senseless animals" as he called them:—

The overseers and workmen employed by Act of Parliament, to make a new road across the kingdom . . . demolish the Wall, and beat the stones in pieces, to make the road withal. Every carving, inscription altar, milestone, pillar, etc., undergoes the same vile havoc, from the hands of these wretches.*

About half a mile beyond Rudchester we notice some old buildings on the south of the road.

Here was once an inn, of which only the outbuildings survive, called "The Iron Sign". It was built almost entirely of Roman stones. The Centurial and sculptured stones (here reproduced from Bruce) which were in a wall of the building are now in the Museum of Antiquities, Newcastle upon Tyne.

---

* Landowners actually complained that more Roman stones were used than was necessary "whereby several parts of the road are higher than should be, and very few, if any, stones are left for making any fence from the new road."

Although difficult to read the first is COH VIII, the second HOS (IDI) LYPI, the third is too obscure.

When we reach the Whittledean Reservoirs at the crossroads to the south stands Welton Tower, a fifteenth century pele built almost entirely of Roman stones. The manor house attached to it has the date 1614 and the initials W.W. (Will of Welton) over the door. Nearly opposite Welton Hall, close behind the wall on the Military Way was found a Roman milestone, now destroyed, whose inscription was preserved in a drawing by John Hodgson. The text is restored by Eric Birley (A.A.4.16). It was set up by the Emperor Antoninus, known as Caracalla, in A.D. 213.

IMP CAES M AVR
[ELIO] ANTONINO
PIO FELICI AVG ARAB
ADIAB P[A]RT MAXIM
O BRIT MAXIMO
TRIB P[OT] XVI COS IIII
IMP II C IVL MARCO
LEG A[V]G P[R] P[R]

As we proceed west little can be seen today and the traveller in Roman times would have seen nothing unusual. As he travelled past the spot where the Robin Hood Inn now stands he would have noted Milecastle 18 which now appears as a low platform south of the road, 150 yards west of Rudchester burn.

RECONSTRUCTION OF A TURRET

Turret 18a (Wallhouses East) was excavated in 1931 and was found to be well preserved with its ladder platform intact. We have attempted a detailed restoration of this turret. There were a number of problems. The first question needing an answer was whether the doors opened inwards or outwards. Roman doors were not hinged like ours but pivot hung. In the turrets at any rate it seems that doors opened outwards.

How many windows were there in a turret? Since the turret was placed at the back of the wall they didn't need to be strong militarily. They were designed for temporary residence. On the ground floor was a hearth where cooking took place. There was no chimney so windows were necessary to allow the smoke to escape and to provide light. A small water tank was set into the soil on the ground floor. The two ground floor windows were unglazed. The window glass which has been found in turrets undoubtedly came from the windows on the first floor. It has been suggested that the first floor was built of wood, an unlikely assumption since the Romans built their military works to last.

Access to the first floor was by a trap door. Originally there was no stair landing (all the stair landings found were later additions) so access must have been by a

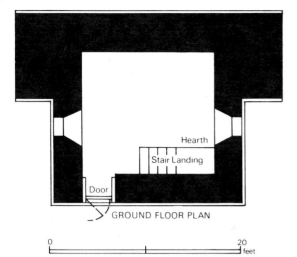

Hearth

Stair Landing

Door

GROUND FLOOR PLAN

0   20
⊢————————————————⊣ feet

ladder against the Wall. Later (perhaps for military security reasons) the fixed ladder was replaced by a moveable one. Without the stair landing the ladder would have had to be about 15 feet long, to raise the store away on the first floor which was only 15 feet from east to west. With the stair landing a shorter ladder of 11 to 12 feet would have been sufficient and easier to store.

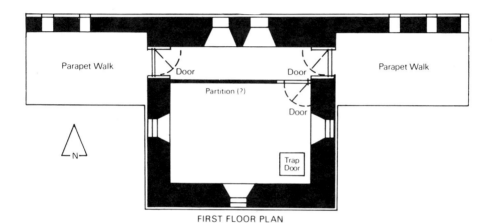

Parapet Walk

Door

Door

Parapet Walk

Partition (?)

Door

N

Trap Door

FIRST FLOOR PLAN

The ground floor was 15 feet high, the same as the parapet walk but the first floor chamber was probably only 10 feet. Besides windows in the east and west walls there was probably one in the south. Since it had access to the parapet walk on both sides it would have been abnormally draughty. This would probably have been avoided by a wooden partition forming a corridor. On the north side of the corridor unglazed windows would have given a view to the north, a great boon for the guards in inclement weather.

Although the upper structure of the turrets and the Wall is entirely conjectural we can assume in the weather prevailing in the north that there was a gabled roof. A flat crenellated top would have been unsuitable for a northern climate. It has been suggested that in the gabled roof there would be a small window in the north gable which would provide a high and wide view to the north.

We do no know how many soldiers were stationed at a turret. The ground floor was undoubtedly used for cooking and the first floor probably provided limited sleeping facilities.

(This section is partly based on an article by Parker Brewis in Archaeologia Aeliana, 1932).

The next Milecastle (19) was also excavated in the same year and an interesting altar discovered (here reproduced). It is 2 feet 6 inches high and one foot square. On the left and right are the customary axe and cleaver. The inscription is as follows (quoted from A.A. 1932 Eric Birley).

Matrib(us) templ(um) cum ara vex (illatio)coh(ortis) I Vard(ullorum), instante P(ublio) D(omitio) V(...)v(otum)s(olvit)l(ibens)m(erito).

"To the Mothers, a vexillation of the first cohort of Vardulli, under Publius Domitius V(ictor) (has erected) a temple with an altar in willing payment of a vow."

The presence of a vexillation from the First Cohort of the Vardulli raises the question of who garrisoned the milecastles and turret since the Vardulli cannot be traced either at Rudchester or Haltonchesters forts. It is usually assumed that the fort garrisons looked after the milecastles. However there are problems in this assumption. Here is one Roman Wall controversy which has not yet been settled.

With a mile to go to Haltonchesters our Roman traveller would have noticed how on Down Hill the Vallum makes a dramatic turn south to avoid the hill which the Wall crosses.

H. Burden Richardson's drawing highlights this change.

HALTONCHESTERS FORT (Onno)

The Roman fort near Halton is called Haltonchesters (in Roman times ONNO). It covers five acres and is divided in two by the modern road. It was garrisoned by a cavalry regiment called the Ala Sabiniana. From Corstopitum it is distant about two and a half miles. It guards Watling Street which traverses the valley immediately beneath it. A portion of a monumental slab, now at Trinity College, Cambridge refers to the fort and its garrison. It is probably a third century inscription. The fort was built between 122 A.D. and 126 A.D.

The Vallum at Down Hill

Size, 1 foot 9 inches by 1 foot 3 inches

(To the Divine Manes)
of Noricus, 30 years of age,
Messorius Magnus
his brother a duplicarius of the
Sabinian wing (placed this).

15

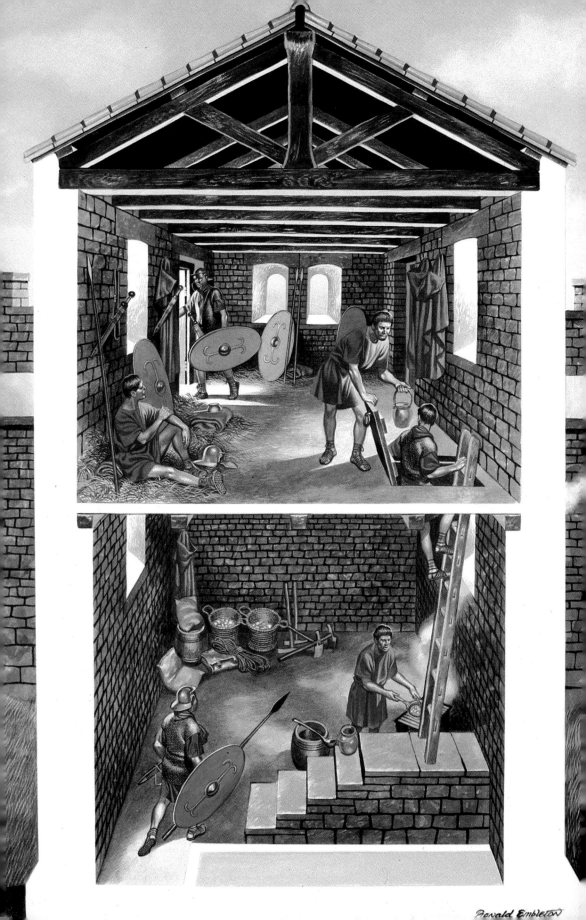

Ronald Embleton

William Hutton is "welcomed" at Rudchester Hall.

he interior of Turret 18A at Wallhouses East

The original Wall and ditch had already been built before the fort had been decided upon. Turret 21a was built 80 yards to the east and turret 21b a similar distance to the west placing them in the unusual position between Milecastles 21 and 22. As soon as the curtain wall was completed a decision to build the fort was taken. The ditch was filled in and turned into a street connecting the east and west gates whose north portals were built on the ditch. A building inscription discovered at the West Gate records the date of the fort.

Dedication slab from West Gate at Haltonchesters fort;

IMP. CAES. Tra Hadriani
AUG. LEG. VI Victrix p.f.
A. PLATORIO Nopate
LEG. AUG. pr. pr.

"To the Emperor Caesar Trajan Hadrian, the Sixth Legion Loyal and Victorious, under Aulus Platorius Nepos, the Emperor's propraetorian Legate." A Platorius Nepos was Imperial Legate in Britain from 122 to C.125.

At a later date (probably in the time of Severus) an extension was built on to the south west side giving the fort an unusual L plan.

When in 1827 the field north of the road (called the "Brunt-ha-penny" field) was first ploughed a fine bath house was discovered. Large internal bath-houses are rare in the Wall forts. In the south part of Hunnum (called Silverhill, probably from the discovery of Roman silver coins) an elaborate slab in Antonine style was discovered. It is here reproduced. The bath-house belongs to the reconstruction under Constantius Chlorus at the end of the third century, when the Severan bath house in the extension was demolished.

18

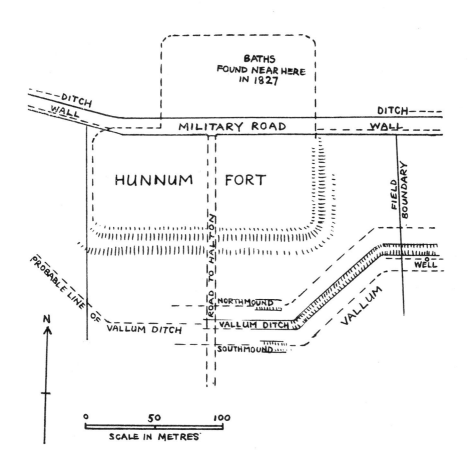

LEG[IO]
SECVNDA
AVG[VSTA]
F[ECIT]

Legion
the second
the august
executed
this work.

The vicus extended for three or five hundred yards south of the fort and it has been suggested the road from the south gate continued south to join Dere Street to the north of Corbridge.

Many inscriptions, tombstones, and sculptures have been found at Haltonchesters. In 1803 a massive gold signet ring was found in the north part of the fort. The woodcut shows its actual size. Its bezel contained a small artificial blue stone on which was engraved a female figure. Probably it belonged to one of the officers who was entitled to wear it. The stone was stolen long ago, and its whereabouts are now unknown.

One of the most interesting buildings discovered at Haltonchesters was a cavalry drill hall. It was 160 feet long an 30 feet wide and spanned the street in front of the Principia. This monumental building was probably built early in the 3rd century. A similar building is recorded at Netherby. We haven't the slightest information about its internal arrangement but can assume it was like a large barn with some lighting in the upper part.

Slavery was a normal feature, in fact the basis of Roman society. Epigraphic evidence for their existence is of course rare since few slaves or their families could afford the expense of a tombstone. This makes the following, found at Haltonchesters, of great interest. It comes from the monument to the slave

Size, 1 foot 8 inches by 1 foot 6 inches.

[D · M ·]
HARDALIO
NIS ·
COLLEGIVM
CONSER
B · M · P ·

[Diis Manibus]
Hardalio-
nis
Collegium
conservo
bene merenti posuit.

Hardalio and was set up by the "guild of his fellow slaves", *colleguim conser (vorum)*. Hardalio is a typical slave name meaning "busybody", and he probably belonged to one of the soldiers stationed here.

How many officers and soldiers had slaves we do not know but probably there were many. We have a number of references to slaves on the Wall. One famous tombstone from South Shields commemorates Regina, the freedwoman and wife of Barates of Palmyre and from the same location we have the fine tombstone to the freedman Victor who was by nationality a Moor but belonged to a cavalryman called Numereanus who came from southern Spain. He was probably bought at one of the slave markets in Britain. The north would be an important source for slaves. In the frequent fighting north of the Wall any prisoners taken would almost certainly be sold into slavery.

Mourners at a Roman Funeral

A Cavalry Drill Hall

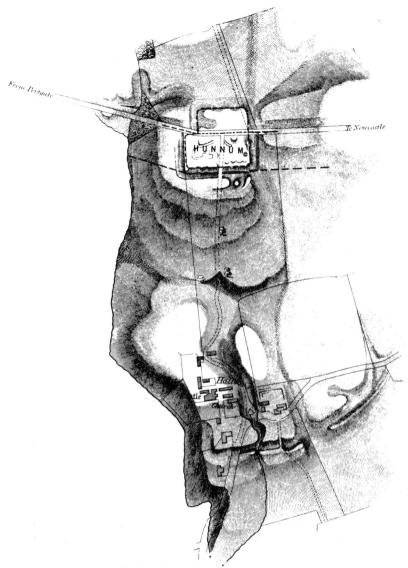

From H. MacLaughlan's "Watling Street," 1857

Receiving the password

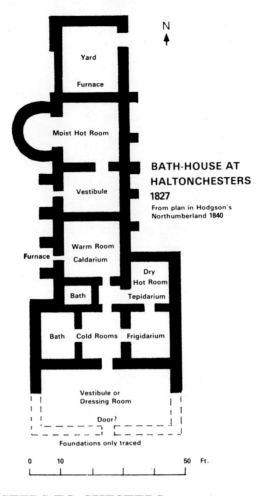

BATH-HOUSE AT HALTONCHESTERS
1827
From plan in Hodgson's
Northumberland 1840

Yard

Furnace

Moist Hot Room

Vestibule

Warm Room
Caldarium

Furnace

Dry
Hot Room

Bath

Tepidarium

Bath   Cold Rooms   Frigidarium

Vestibule or
Dressing Room

Door?

Foundations only traced

0   10   50   Ft.

HALTONCHESTERS TO CHESTERS

On leaving Haltonchesters we cross the Fence burn and climb the hill which brings us to Milecastle 22. Its north gate was blocked towards the end of the 2nd century because the gate at Portgate served the same purpose. At Portgate, 260 yards farther on, Dere Street crossed the Wall. It was first described by Horsley as a "square structure half within and half without" the Wall. It lies south west of the new Errington Arms roundabout just north of the old road before the roundabout was built.

CHO · VIII

> C A E C I L I

CLIIME

Cohortis octavæ
centuria Cæcilii
Clementis.

Size, 1 foot 3 inches by 9 inches.

*A centurial stone in the front of the farmhouse at St. Oswald's Hill Head. It reads –
"the century of Caecilius Clemens of the eighth cohort".*

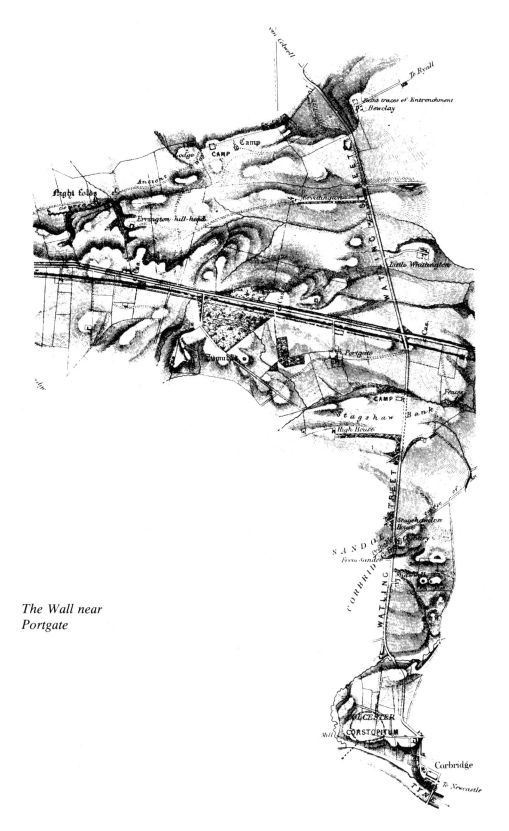

The Wall near Portgate

ROMAN FAIR

At Stagshaw Bank between Corbridge and the Roman Wall on Dere Street was once held a great fair whose origins are shrouded in antiquity. Today it is difficult to visualize the bustle of this great fair with the great multitude which attended. It is very likely this cattle fair has its origin in Roman times. About one mile west of Haltonchesters the Roman road Dere Street crossed the Wall at Portgate. Dere Street was a military road but was also used by traders since it passed through the whole of Northumberland and into Scotland it would have been ideal for the movement of cattle. The Roman Wall garrison and the thousands of civilians who lived in the vicinity along the Wall would provide a ready market for any surplus cattle reared in the native settlements of which there were many in the relatively peaceful hills and plains of Northumberland.

So a fair would have been an ideal place where the agricultural products of the north could be exchanged for the various products of the more civilised south, such as pottery, metal work, leather goods and clothes.

Two hundred yards beyond Portgate near turret 22A the slab here illustrated was found.

J. STOREY DEL   JD UTTING SC

The inscription FYLGVR. DIVO(RV)M meaning the *lightning of the Gods* suggests some soldier was here hit by a lightning bolt. When passing the superstitious Roman soldier or traveller would make some religious sign to ward off from himself any such calamity.

Five hundred yards further on we find the Vallum in a remarkable state of preservation.

Hutton's description of these earthworks has often been quoted:

I now travel over a large common, still upon the Wall, with its trench nearly complete. But what was my surprise when I beheld, thirty yards on my left, the united works of Agricola and Hadrian, almost perfect! I climbed over a stone wall to examine the wonder; measured the whole in every direction; surveyed them with surprise, with delight; was fascinated, and unable to proceed; forgot I was upon a wild common, a stranger, and the evening approaching. I had the grandest works under my eye of the greatest men of the age in which they lived, and of the most eminent nation then existing; all of which had suffered but little during the long course of sixteen hundred years. Even hunger and fatigue were lost in the grandeur before me. If a man writes a book upon a turnpike-road, he cannot be expected to move quick; but, lost in astonishment, I was not able to move at all.

Ronald Embleton

South of milecastle 24 is a Roman quarry, one of several found near the Wall. Here on Fallowfield Fell was the famous Written Rock carved on a large ridge of

sandstone, carrying in deeply chiselled letters the inscription PETRA FLAVI(I) CARANTINI. It is thought that Flavius Carantinus may have been the foreman of the gang who were quarrying stones for the Wall.

Ronald Embleton

There are other rocks inscribed by soldiers working in the Wall quarries but this one is the most famous and to preserve it from vandals has been removed to Chesters Museum.

Opposite. The Roman gate at Postgate.

The Turret at Brunton

The Wall at Brunton

Our Roman traveller approaching Chesters in his day wouldn't have noticed anything special but today our Wall pilgrim for the first time since Heddon on the Wall would see part of the Wall still standing, a very fine section indeed, which owes its preservation to William Hutton who almost two centuries ago arrived as the farmer was demolishing it. Due to Hutton's remonstrances part was left standing.

Here also today we can visit Brunton Turret, one of the best preserved on the line of the Wall, standing fourteen courses high. Here we can see the change in the width of the Wall.

At Brunton Turret the Wall is 9 feet 3 inches thick but there is no abrupt expansion but a gradual thickening of the Wall as it reaches the turret. About 50 yards west of the turret the Wall is 7 feet 10 inches thick. This increase in the width of the Wall near the turret bears some relation to the passage of the rampart walk over the lower chamber of the turret. It also effects the upper structure of the turret which of course has now gone. The core of the Wall is now mortared for preservation but originally was set in puddled clay which was still resilient when uncovered in 1950. In front of the Wall the ditch is very bold.

From Brunton Turret the Wall ran in a straight line to the North Tyne where the soldiers crossed by the magnificent stone bridge at which our Roman traveller would have been as amazed as we are by the Humber and the Forth bridges. For its time the bridge at Chesters was probably a greater feat of engineerng.

HADRIAN'S WALL IN THE DAYS OF THE ROMANS
by Ronald Embleton and Frank Graham

The present book is part of a much larger work which has been in preparation for fifteen years and we hope to publish in 1984. The book will contain approximately 80 full page colour plates and 300 illustrations in black and white. It will show what the Wall was like when in use, describing the soldiers who built and garrisoned it.

Every aspect of Roman life will be illustrated with reconstructions, not only of buildings but of the everyday life of the soldiers and civilians. Never before has such a grand attempt been made to show in vivid colourful details the life of Roman Britain.

The drawings by Ronald Embleton have already attracted world-wide notice and are acknowledged to be among the best reconstructions of Roman life both from an artistic and historical viewpoint.

We would be pleased if our readers would not make enquiries until the book appears when it will be well advertised. The retail price will, we hope, be approximately £12.

A Roman Surveyor